EASY PIANO

Christmas Songs FOR KIDS

ISBN 978-1-70510-291-6

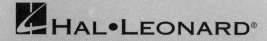

HAL•LEONARD®

Visit Hal Leonard Online at
www.halleonard.com

Contact us:
Hal Leonard
7777 West Bluemound Road
Milwaukee, WI 53213
Email: info@halleonard.com

In Europe, contact:
Hal Leonard Europe Limited
42 Wigmore Street
Marylebone, London, W1U 2RN
Email: info@halleonardeurope.com

In Australia, contact:
Hal Leonard Australia Pty. Ltd.
4 Lentara Court
Cheltenham, Victoria, 3192 Australia
Email: info@halleonard.com.au

CONTENTS

✳

Song Notes

All I Want for Christmas Is You

This Christmas love song from the 1990s is one of the most popular modern Christmas songs ever recorded. With an upbeat and energetic style, keep the quarter notes moving after the opening measures. Create a little dramatic flair with the fermatas in measure 10, and then settle into a groove with the triplets in measure 11. The tempo is "Moderately" but don't play too slowly. Choose your tempo based on the quarter notes returning in measure 15.

Believe

This beautiful ballad first performed by Josh Groban is from the 2004 holiday film *Polar Express*. The melody moves through leaping intervals but should be played legato and in a lyrical style. The left-hand accompaniment moves slowly, mostly whole-note and half-note rhythms. When the melody moves in eighth notes on page 10 be careful not to rush. Singing along will help you stay steady.

The Chipmunk Song

This fun favorite from 1958 is so popular it reached #1 on the Billboard Hot 100. That distinctive chipmunk sound on the recording was achieved by recording the vocals at varying speeds. No matter your favorite Chipmunk (Alvin, Simon, or Theodore), launch right into this tune with plenty of energy. Note the $\frac{3}{4}$ time signature, but instead of counting individual quarter-note beats, think bigger, with one beat per measure, really swinging along. Whenever you play the left-hand passing notes, bring those out for even more forward movement.

The Christmas Song (Chestnuts Roasting on an Open Fire)

Nat King Cole is the vocalist most associated with this classic song, written in 1945. The melody begins with an octave leap, so be ready to stretch from middle C to the next higher C, cascading down the scale like a sled on a snowy hill. Don't let the accidentals (sharps and flats not in the key signature) worry you. The tempo of this song is slow, and you'll have plenty of time to look ahead for all the changes.

Christmas Time Is Here

From the holiday television special *A Charlie Brown Christmas*, this Vince Guaraldi jazz tune has a slow, lyrical feel. Don't rush the quarter-note beat, but let it be the steady pulse that moves the melody forward. Look ahead for accidentals, sharps and flats not in the key signature. In measure 29 you'll see the word, "Instrumental." The lyrics take a break here, coming back with "Sleighbells in the air…" and continuing to the end of the song.

Do You Hear What I Hear

This song about the Nativity has been covered by hundreds of artists, perhaps most famously by Bing Crosby in 1963. Study the music, looking for patterns and repetitions. For example, measures 1–2 are almost the same as measures 3–4. The left-hand measures 5–8 are repeated in measures 9–12 and several more times. Phrases in the right-hand melody repeat as well. Compare the last four measures with the introduction. What do you notice?

Feliz Navidad

This 1970s Christmas hit by singer/songwriter José Feliciano has a Spanish chorus and an English verse. "Feliz Navidad" is the traditional Puerto Rican Christmas greeting, "Merry Christmas, a prosperous year and happiness." Spend some time working with the left hand alone. The syncopation in the bass clef is what this song is all about. Count steady quarter notes as you work through the rhythms, and let this part shine, bringing it out a bit against the longer, tied notes in the right hand.

Frosty the Snow Man

Sung by Jimmy Durante in the 1969 animated TV special *Frosty the Snow Man*, this bouncy holiday favorite is hard to play without a smile on your face. "Swing" the eighth notes but keep a steady quarter-note beat throughout. Notice the triplet figures, first in the right hand, then in the left hand, and play them with a jaunty flourish.

Happy Holiday

The crooner Bing Crosby first sang "Happy Holiday" in the classic 1942 Christmas film *Holiday Inn*. The opening motive on the words "Happy Holiday" appears throughout the song. This rhythm, four eighth notes followed by a half note, really shape the song. Note the designation to "swing" the eighth notes, so don't play that rhythm straight. Just swing it gently and let this holiday wish sing out.

Here Comes Santa Claus (Right Down Santa Claus Lane)

It's believed cowboy legend Gene Autry got the idea for this song while riding his horse in a holiday parade in 1946, hearing the crowd exclaim, "Here Comes Santa Claus." He was the first to perform the song, with music composed by Oakley Haldeman, in 1947. It was a Top 10 hit on both the pop and country charts and remains a Christmas favorite. Right hand begins the melody on middle C. Reach up with finger 5 to play the first interval, a 6th. In measure 3, reach a little farther with finger 5, to play a 7th, and then in measure 7, stretch from middle C to the next highest C, an octave. Left hand plays a steady pattern of quarter notes and rests, so settle in and enjoy all four verses of this classic.

A Holly Jolly Christmas

This popular holiday tune was featured in the 1964 television special *Rudolph the Red-Nosed Reindeer*, sung by Burl Ives as the character Sam the Snowman. Studying the intervals (distance between two notes on the staff and keyboard) is helpful when learning this song. For example, in right-hand measures 1–2, you'll see a 6th moving to a 5th, moving to a 4th. Notice that for all three intervals the bottom note E stays the same, only the top note changes. In measures 5–6 the note F stays constant, and in measure 7, the B stays constant. Continue looking for intervals in this way throughout the song.

I Saw Mommy Kissing Santa Claus

Another favorite from the 1950s, this tune has been covered by numerous artists over the years, perhaps most famously by The Jackson 5. The melody encompasses an octave, so note the fingering provided to enable you to play with a smooth, connected sound. The left hand starts out with tied whole notes, so be sure to hold those notes for their full value. Keep an eye out for accidentals in both hands; they give the song its colorful harmony.

I'll Be Home for Christmas

Recorded in 1943 by Bing Crosby, this emotional tune was written to honor soldiers overseas in World War II. It became a Top 10 hit and remains a Christmas standard. Play this tune in a smooth, lyrical style, moderately, not too slow, as indicated. Note that each four-measure phrase concludes with left-hand passing notes, creating a bit of a counter-melody against the right-hand tied notes. Bring out those left-hand notes in the same singing style as the right hand.

It's Beginning to Look Like Christmas

This 1950s favorite has been sung and recorded by many artists over the years. It remains popular, most recently covered in the 2000s by Michael Bublé and acapella group Pentatonix. The familiar hook of this tune is heard right away, in the introduction. The triplet followed by dotted eighth-sixteenth defines this song; spend a little time getting comfortable playing it smoothly. These two rhythms (triplet and dotted eighth) figure prominently throughout the song, so once you have those rhythms solid, the rest of the song will be easy to play.

Let It Snow! Let It Snow! Let It Snow!

This "snowy" tune has been popular at the holidays since it was written in 1945. The melody gets its bounce from a feeling of two beats per measure, as notated by the time signature designating cut time. Notice that the left hand begins in treble clef, creating a nifty duet with the right hand. This happens again in measures 8–9, and in the last line of the song.

A Marshmallow World

As the tempo suggests, you'll want to play this popular wintertime song with a lilt, swinging the eighth notes in the right-hand melody. Written in 1949 and often associated with Christmas, it's interesting to note the lyrics make no mention of the holidays. Bring out the triplets in measures 8, 10, 18, and 26 for a fun flourish.

Mary, Did You Know?

This modern Christmas song was first recorded in 1991. Since then it's reached the Billboard Top 10 multiple times, sung by various artists in many different styles. The poignant melody is gentle and slow, but with a good amount of syncopation. Count aloud at first to get a feel for where the strong beats fall. In contrast, the left hand plays a simple accompaniment, allowing you to let the melody shine.

The Most Wonderful Time of the Year

The iconic American singer Andy Williams recorded this cheery holiday tune in 1963. The $\frac{3}{4}$ time signature gives this classic a waltz-like feel, with a slight accent on beat one of each measure. Choose a moderately fast tempo to keep the melody moving. In measures 29–32 (after the 2nd ending), there's a neat chromatic passage in the left hand. Chromatic notes move by half steps (on the piano, one key to the very next key, white or black) so take a minute to practice that spot ahead of time, to highlight this fun series of passing notes.

Rockin' Around the Christmas Tree

Brenda Lee was only 13 years old when she recorded this Johnny Marks favorite in 1958. Right from the introduction there's a rock 'n' roll groove, so give the syncopation in the right hand a little extra emphasis. The left-hand chimes in with a bit of syncopation in the accompaniment too, so keep the groove going as the attention shifts from hand to hand. Sing along for even more holiday fun!

Rudolph the Red-Nosed Reindeer

This holiday favorite was written by Johnny Marks and sung by Gene Autry in 1949. Play the iconic opening "freely" and swing the eighth notes once you start measure 9. Use the familiar lyrics to help you with the syncopated rhythm: eighth-quarter-eighth. There's a playful two-measure ending, so keep the tempo in time and have fun with the staccatos for a brilliant finish.

Santa Claus Is Comin' to Town

One of the oldest Christmas songs to top the charts, this favorite was first recorded in 1934 and became an instant hit, recorded by over 200 artists over the decades. Studying the form of this song will help you learn it quickly. After a two-measure intro (don't forget to add a dramatic pause on the fermata!), look at the next eight measures (m. 3–10). Let's call this section A. Compare this with the next eight measures (m. 11–18). They're the same. The next eight measures (m. 19–26) are different, so we'll call this section B. Are the last eight measures like section A, section B, or altogether different? If you said section A, you are correct. The form of this song is: AABA.

Silver Bells

"Silver Bells" was recorded in 1950 and sung by Bob Hope and Marilyn Maxwell in the motion picture *The Lemon Drop Kid*. Set a flowing tempo, noting the $\frac{3}{4}$ time signature, as this first section leads to the familiar lyrics, "City sidewalks, busy sidewalks…" At the chorus (measure 33) there's a bit of an echo effect in the right hand. Note the 8va sign, which indicates that those notes are played an octave higher. Practice moving up the octave and back until you can do so comfortably while maintaining a steady beat.

Somewhere in My Memory

This gentle holiday song was composed by John Williams for the popular 1990 Christmas comedy, *Home Alone*. You'll hear it throughout the film as part of the score and sung in its entirety. Really sing out with the right hand as you play this lyrical melody. Balance the left-hand accompaniment carefully. Be aware of the continuous two-note chords throughout; they should stay quietly supporting, with a full, round tone.

Underneath the Tree

Co-written and sung by pop star Kelly Clarkson, this cheery tune debuted in 2013. Think of ringing holiday bells as you play the introduction. Count through the first eight measures of the melody at a slow tempo first. You'll notice those rhythms repeat. Increase your tempo as you feel comfortable with both notes and rhythms. Do the same for the verses (starting in measure 21). When you're ready, let this up-tempo holiday hit go!

White Christmas

One of the most classic holiday songs, "White Christmas" was written by Irving Berlin and sung by Bing Crosby in 1941. This beautiful ballad requires careful attention to detail. You may consider learning each hand alone at first. In the right hand, pay attention to the fingering to achieve a singing, legato tone. The left-hand part often requires the bass note to be held through or into the next measure while an upper line is played. In measure 7, keep the D held while the middle C is played. In measure 11, hold the E while the quarter notes are played. Listen for the middle voice to sing out, but not overpower the melody note above. The second ending brings this sentimental ballad to a close with downward flowing quarter notes. Be careful here—right hand starts on high B; left hand starts on D above middle C.

Believe

from Warner Bros. Pictures' THE POLAR EXPRESS

Words and Music by GLEN BALLARD
and ALAN SILVESTRI

Moderately slow

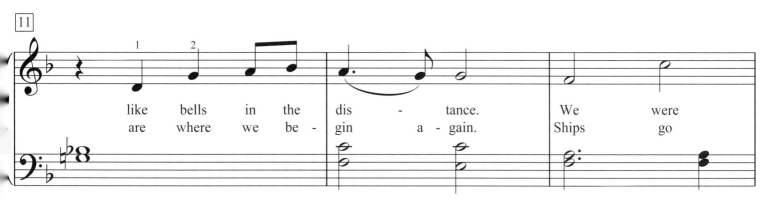

14

dream - ers / sail - ing   not so long a - / far a - cross the   go, _____ / sea, _____

17

but one by / trust - ing   one, we / star - light   to get where they   all had to

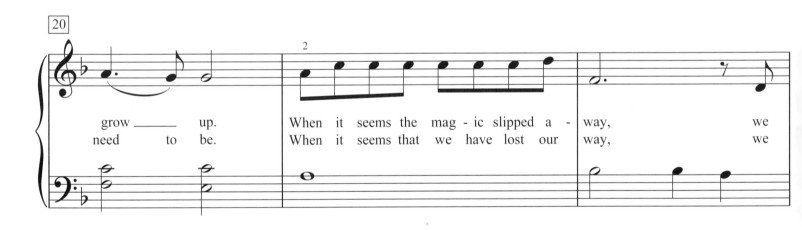

20

grow _____ up. / need to be.   When it seems the mag - ic slipped a - / When it seems that we have lost our   way, / way,   we / we

23

find it all a - gain on Christ - mas / find our - selves a - gain on Christ - mas   Day. / Day.   Be - lieve in what your heart is say - ing,

26

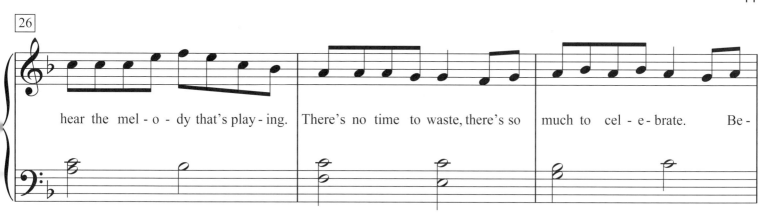

hear the mel - o - dy that's play - ing. There's no time to waste, there's so much to cel - e - brate. Be -

29

lieve in what you feel in - side and give your dreams the wings to fly.

32

1.

You have ev - 'ry - thing you need if you just ___ be - lieve.

36

2.

___ be - lieve. *rit.*

All I Want for Christmas Is You

Words and Music by MARIAH CAREY
and WALTER AFANASIEFF

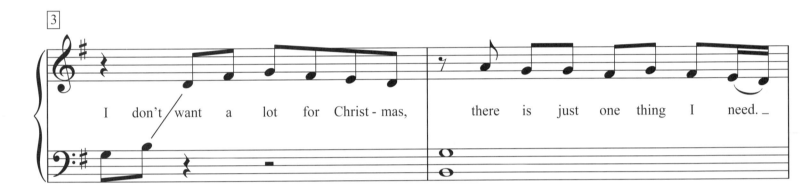

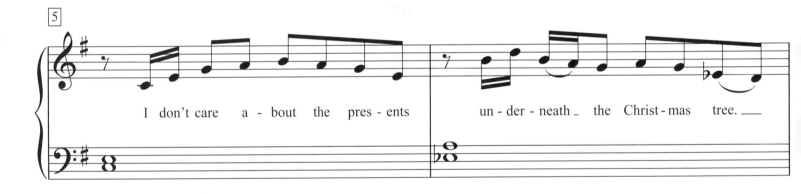

Make my wish come true: ___ all I ___ want for Christ-mas is you. ___

Moderately (♩♩ = ♩ ♪)

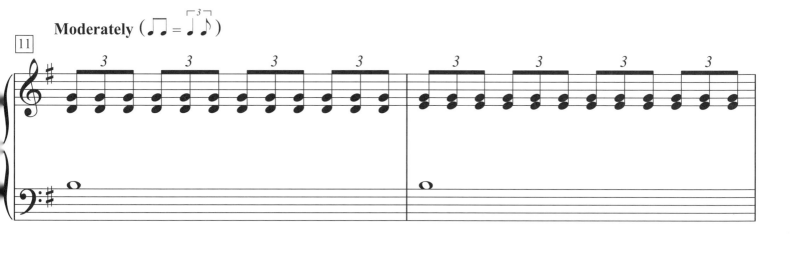

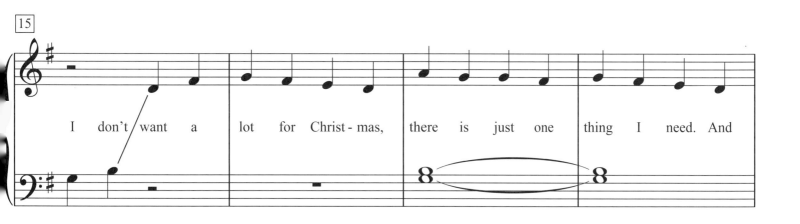

I don't want a lot for Christ-mas, there is just one thing I need. And

I don't care a - bout the pres - ents un - der - neath the Christ - mas tree. ___

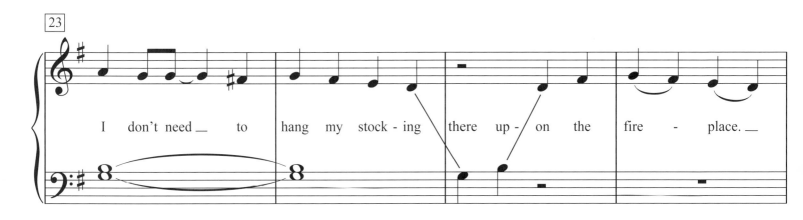

I don't need ___ to hang my stock - ing there up - on the fire - place. ___

San - ta Claus won't make me hap - py with a toy on Christ - mas day. ___

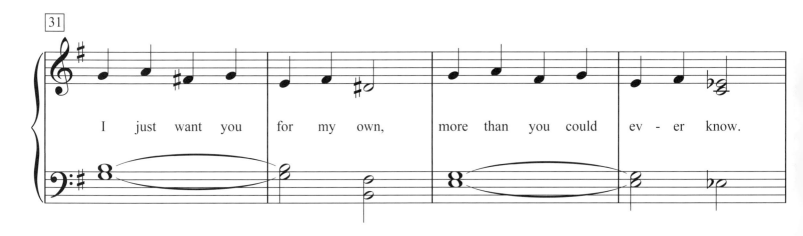

I just want you for my own, more than you could ev - er know.

Make my wish come true. _____ Ba - by, all I want for Christ - mas _____

_____ is _____ you. _____

Oo, _____ ba - by. _____ All I want for Christ - mas is

you, _____ ba - by. _____ ba - by. _____

The Chipmunk Song

Words and Music by
ROSS BAGDASARIAN

Happily

Christ - mas, Christ - mas time is near,

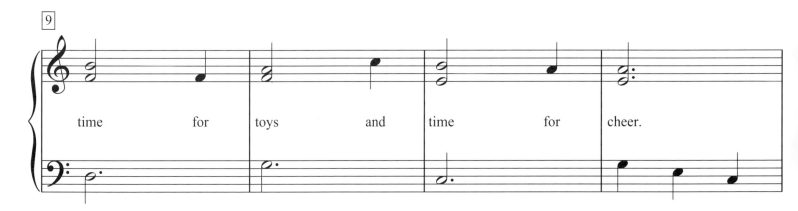

time for toys and time for cheer.

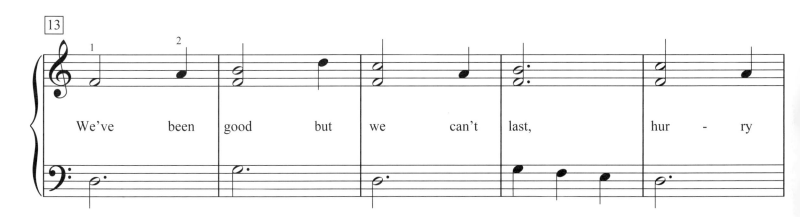

We've been good but we can't last, hur - ry

Christ - mas, hur - ry fast! Want a plane that

loops the loop; me, I want a hu - la

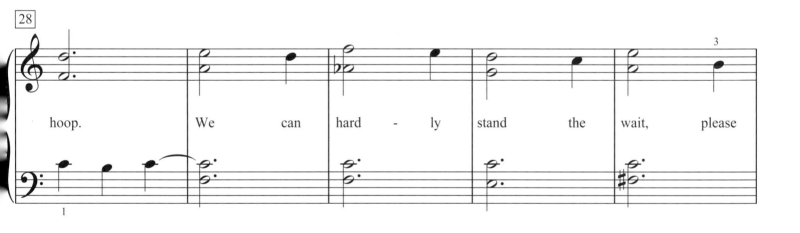

hoop. We can hard - ly stand the wait, please

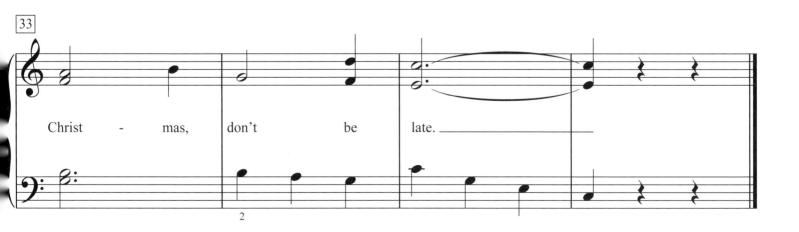

Christ - mas, don't be late. _____

The Christmas Song
(Chestnuts Roasting on an Open Fire)

Music and Lyric by MEL TORMÉ
and ROBERT WELLS

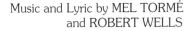

Slowly

Chest - nuts roast - ing on an o - pen fire, Jack Frost nip - ping at your

nose, Yule - tide car - ols be - ing sung by a choir and

folks dressed up like Es - ki - mos. Ev - 'ry - bod - y

knows a tur - key and some mis - tle - toe help to make the sea - son

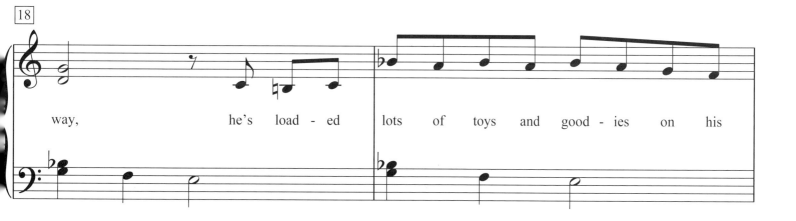

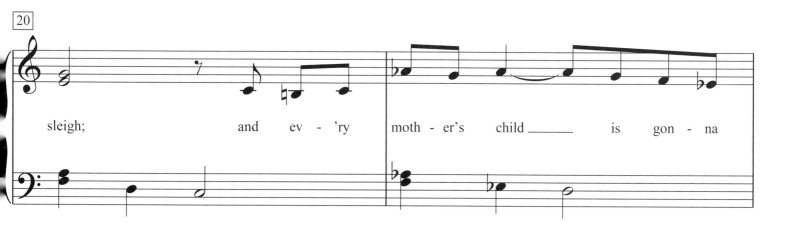

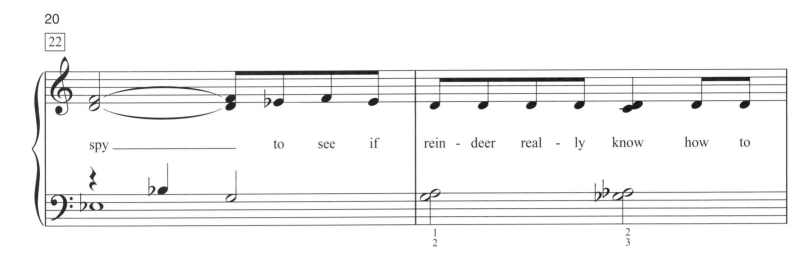

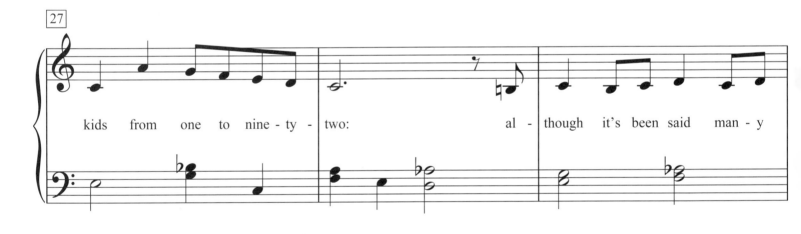

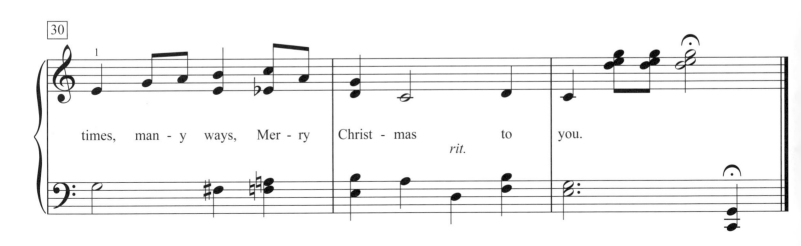

Christmas Time Is Here

from A CHARLIE BROWN CHRISTMAS

Words by LEE MENDELSON
Music by VINCE GUARALDI

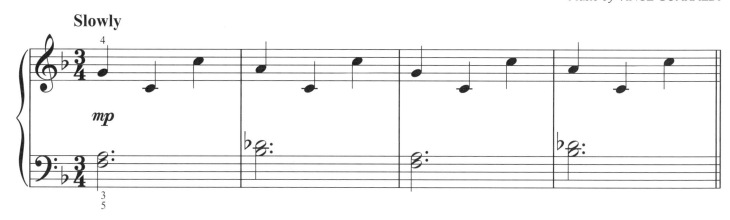

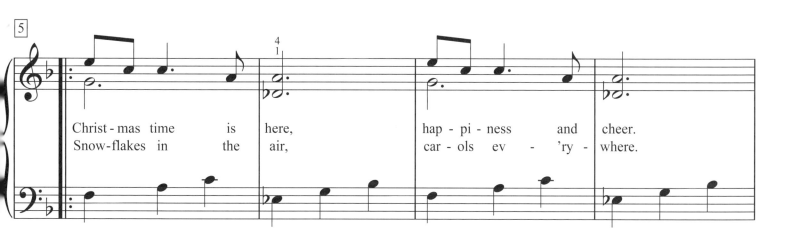

Christ - mas time is here, hap - pi - ness and cheer.
Snow - flakes in the air, car - ols ev - 'ry - where.

Fun for all that chil - dren call their fa - v'rite time of year.
Old - en times and an - cient rhymes of love and dreams to

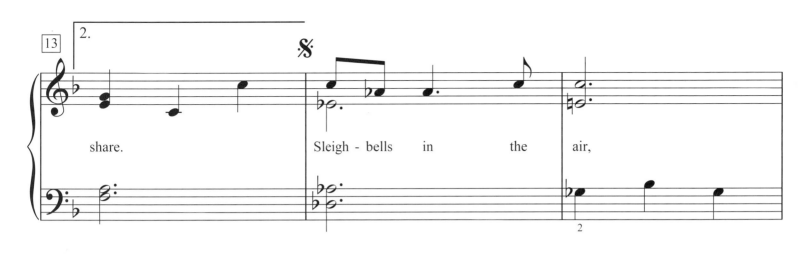

share. Sleigh - bells in the air,

beau - ty ev - 'ry - where. Yule - tide by the

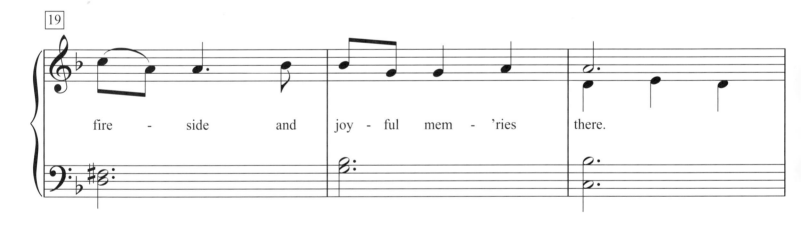

fire - side and joy - ful mem - 'ries there.

Christ-mas time is here, we'll be draw - ing near.

To Coda ⊕

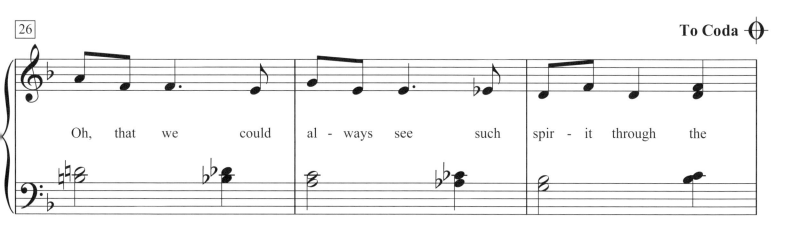

Oh, that we could al - ways see such spir - it through the

year. *Instrumental*

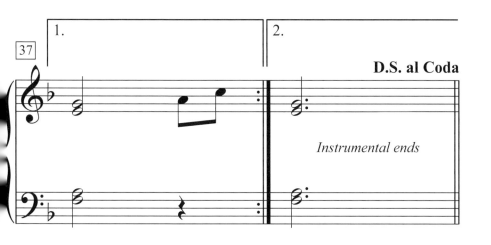

D.S. al Coda

Instrumental ends

CODA ⊕

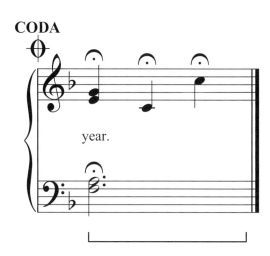

year.

Do You Hear What I Hear

Words and Music by NOEL REGNEY
and GLORIA SHAYNE

star, a star, danc-ing in the night, with a tail as big as a
song, a song, high a-bove the tree, with a voice as big as the
Child, a Child shiv-ers in the cold; let us bring Him sil-ver and

kite, with a tail as big as a kite."
sea, with a voice as big as the sea."
gold, let us bring Him sil-ver and gold."

1., 2.

Said the
Said the

3.

Said the king to the peo-ple ev-'ry

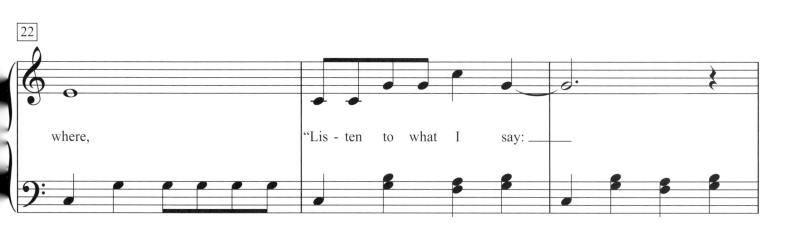

where, "Lis-ten to what I say: ____

Pray for peace, peo - ple ev - 'ry - where! Lis - ten to what I say: ___

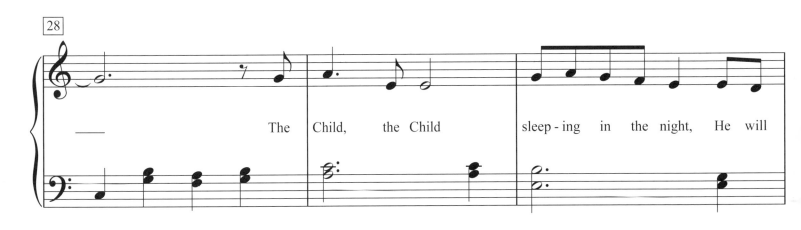

___ The Child, the Child sleep - ing in the night, He will

bring us good - ness and light, He will bring us good - ness and

light! *rall.*

Happy Holiday

from the Motion Picture Irving Berlin's HOLIDAY INN

Words and Music by
IRVING BERLIN

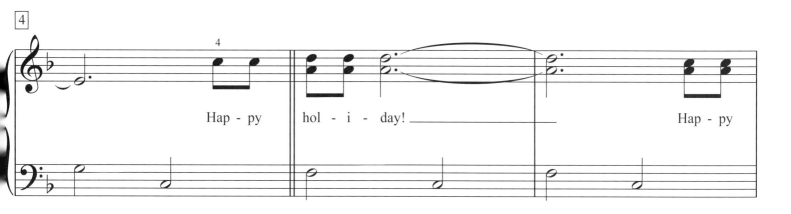

Hap - py hol - i - day! _____ Hap - py

hol - i - day! _____ While the mer - ry bells keep

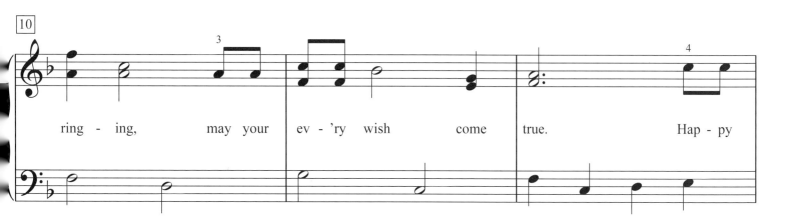

ring - ing, may your ev - 'ry wish come true. Hap - py

13

hol - i - day! _____ Hap - py hol - i - day! _____

16

_____ May the cal - en - dar keep bring - ing hap - py

19

hol - i - days to you. Hap - py hol - i - day! _____

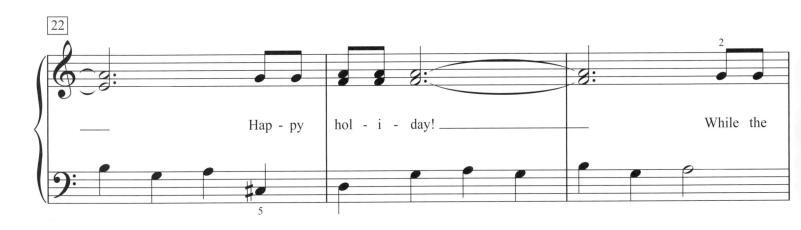

22

_____ Hap - py hol - i - day! _____ While the

merry bells keep ringing, may your ev-'ry wish come

true. Hap-py hol-i-day! Hap-py

hol-i-day! May the cal-en-dar keep

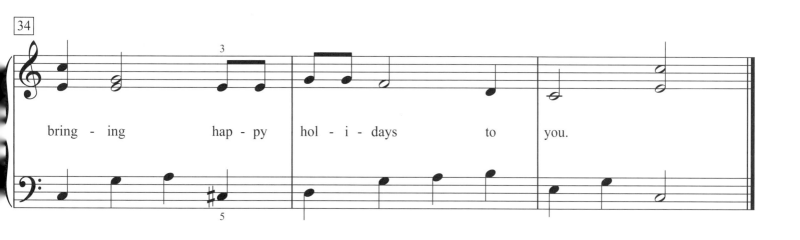

bring-ing hap-py hol-i-days to you.

Feliz Navidad

Music and Lyrics by
JOSÉ FELICIANO

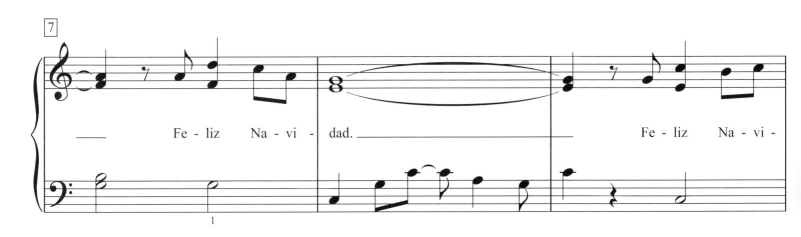

22

heart. _____ I want to wish you a Mer - ry Christ-mas

25

with mis - tle - toe and ___ lots of cheer, ___ with lots of laugh-ter through-

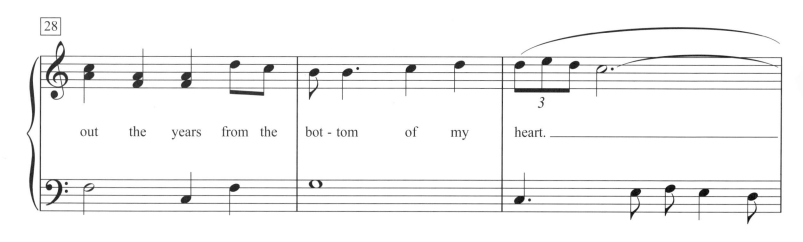

28

out the years from the bot - tom of my heart. _____

31

D.S. al Coda

___ Fe - liz Na - vi -

CODA

A Holly Jolly Christmas

Music and Lyrics by
JOHNNY MARKS

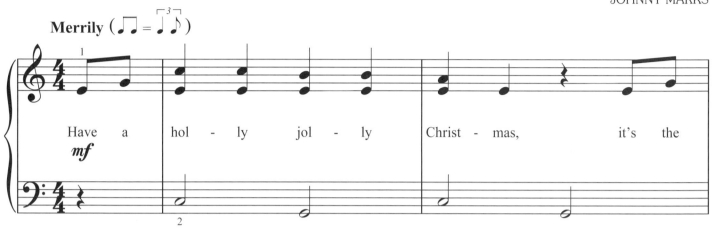

Have a hol - ly jol - ly Christ - mas, it's the

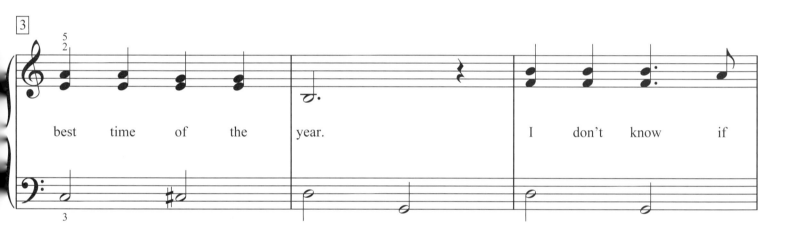

best time of the year. I don't know if

there'll be snow, but let's all give a cheer. Have a

Some - bod - y waits for you, kiss her once for

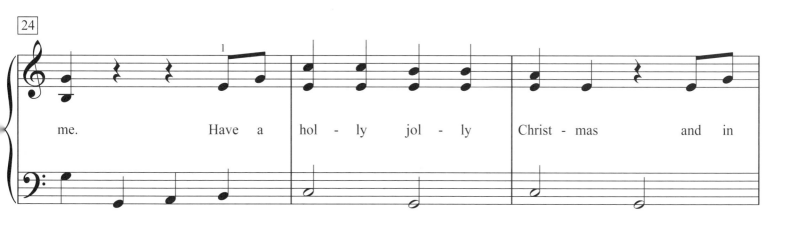

me. Have a hol - ly jol - ly Christ - mas and in

case you did - n't hear, oh by gol - ly, have a

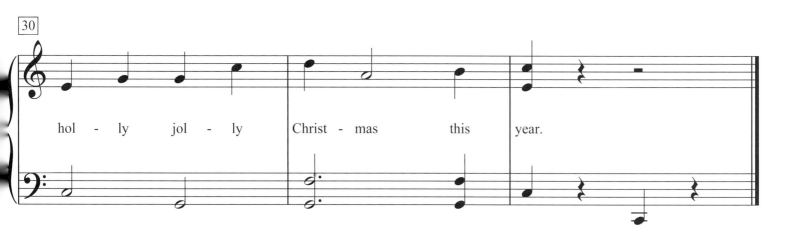

hol - ly jol - ly Christ - mas this year.

Frosty the Snow Man

Words and Music by STEVE NELSON
and JACK ROLLINS

Frost - y the Snow Man was a
Frost - y the Snow Man knew the

jol - ly hap - py soul, with a corn - cob pipe and a
sun was hot that day. So he said, "Let's run and we'll

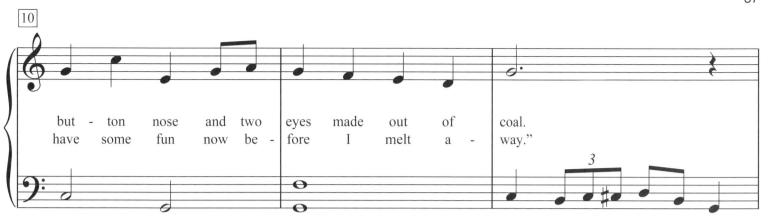

but - ton nose and two eyes made out of coal.
have some fun now be - fore I melt a - way."

Frost - y the Snow Man is a fair - y tale they
Down to the vil - lage is with a broom - stick in his

say; he was made of snow, but the chil - dren know how he
hand, run - ning here and there all a - round the square, say - in',

came to life one day. There must have been some
"Catch me if you can." He led them down the

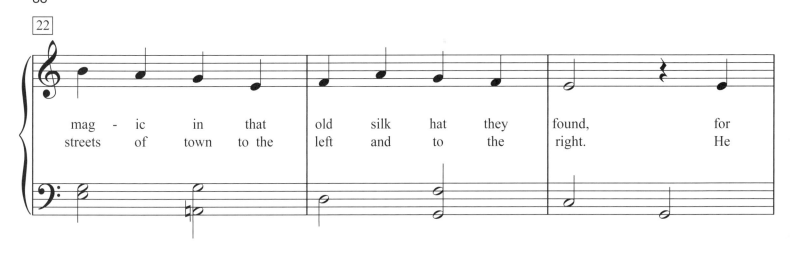

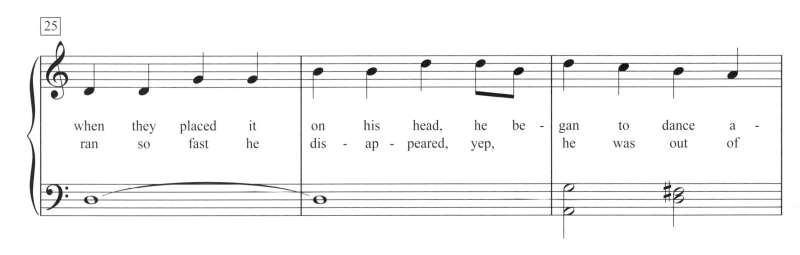

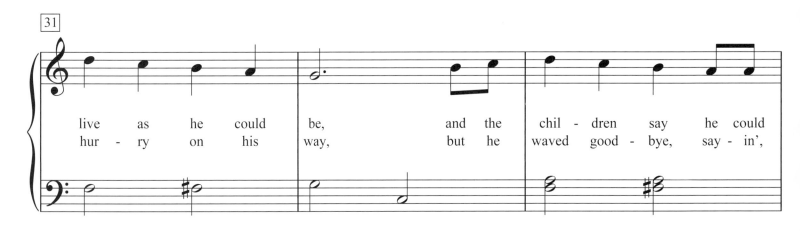

Here Comes Santa Claus
(Right Down Santa Claus Lane)

Words and Music by GENE AUTRY
and OAKLEY HALDEMAN

Moderately bright

Here comes San-ta Claus! Here comes San-ta Claus!

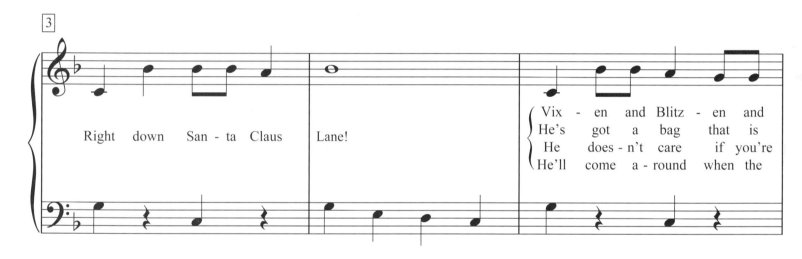

Right down San-ta Claus Lane!

Vix - en and Blitz - en and
He's got a bag that is
He does - n't care if you're
He'll come a - round when the

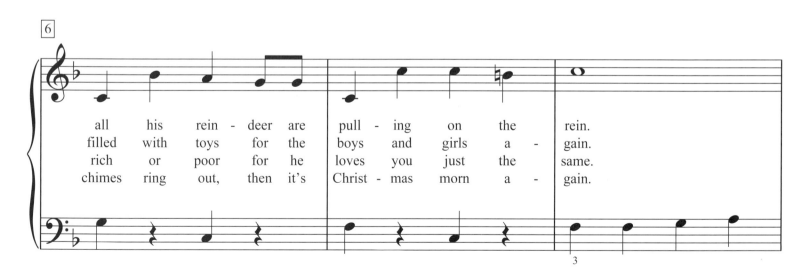

all his rein - deer are pull - ing on the rein.
filled with toys for the boys and girls a - gain.
rich or poor for he loves you just the same.
chimes ring out, then it's Christ - mas morn a - gain.

Bells are ring - ing, chil - dren sing - ing, all is mer - ry and
Hear those sleigh - bells jin - gle jan - gle, what a beau - ti - ful
San - ta knows that we're God's chil - dren, that makes ev - 'ry - thing
Peace on earth will come to all if we just fol - low the

bright.
sight.   Hang your stock - ings and say your pray'rs,
right.   Jump in bed, cov - er up your head, ⎫ 'cause
light.   Fill your hearts with a Christ - mas cheer, ⎬
                Let's give thanks to the Lord a - bove, ⎭

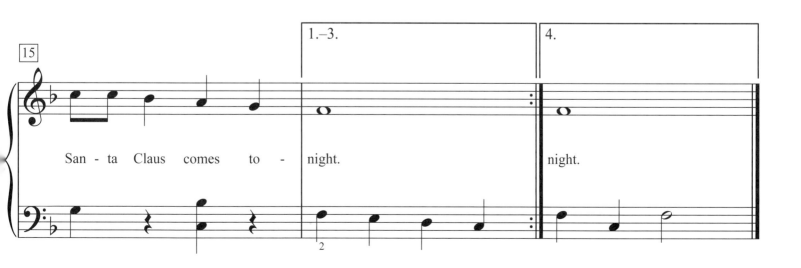

Santa Claus comes to - night.

night.

I Saw Mommy Kissing Santa Claus

Words and Music by
TOMMIE CONNOR

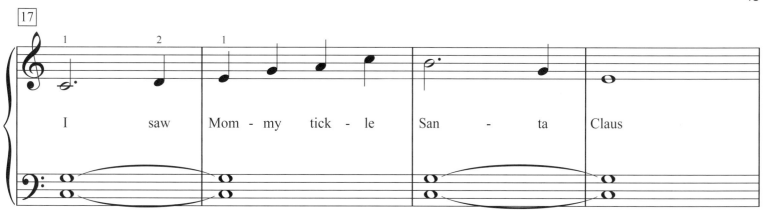

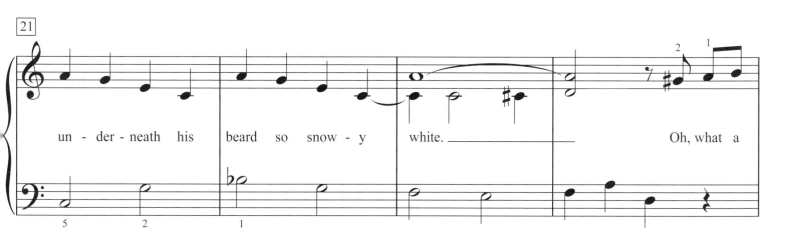

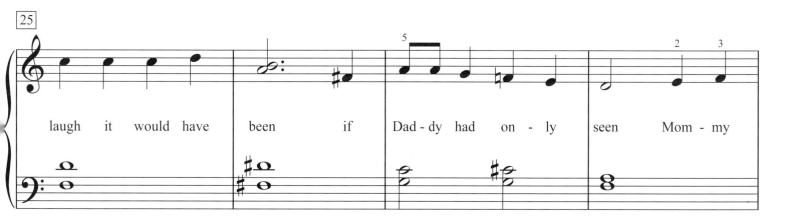

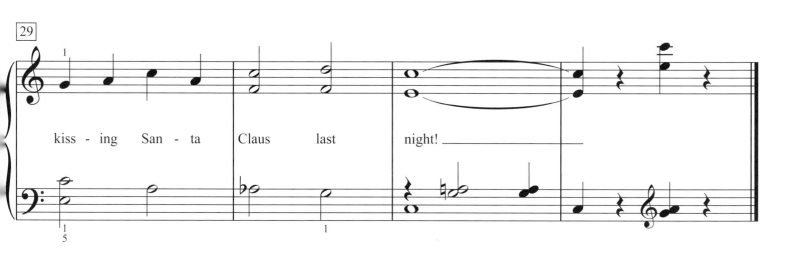

I'll Be Home for Christmas

Words and Music by KIM GANNON
and WALTER KENT

Moderately, in 2

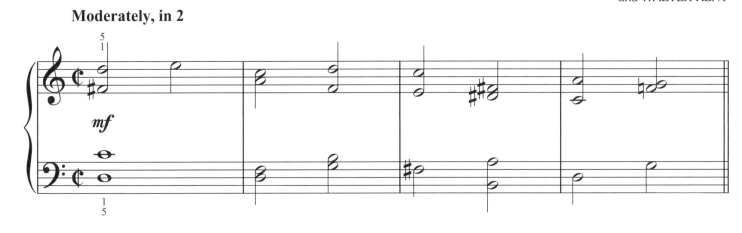

I'll   be   home   for   Christ - mas. _____   You   can

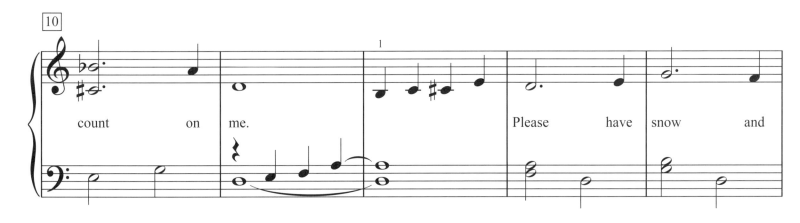

count   on   me.   Please   have   snow   and

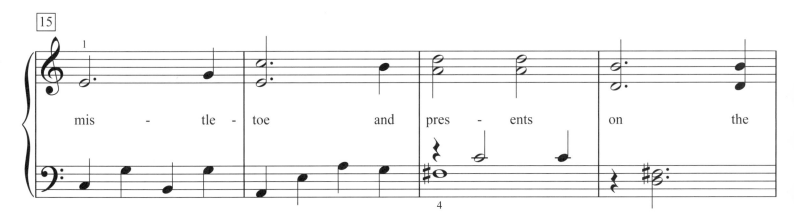

mis - tle - toe   and   pres - ents   on   the

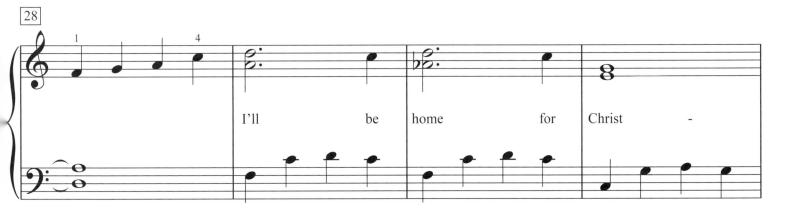

It's Beginning to Look Like Christmas

By MEREDITH WILLSON

gin-ning to look a lot like Christ - mas, ev - 'ry-where you go. Take a look in the five and ten, glis-ten-ing once a-gain, with can - dy canes and sil - ver lanes a - glow. It's be -

gin-ning to look a lot like Christ - mas, toys in ev - 'ry

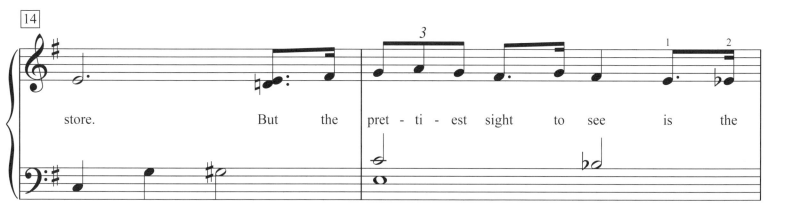

store. But the pret - ti - est sight to see is the

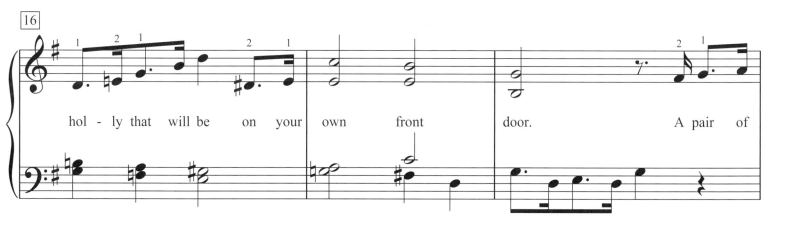

hol - ly that will be on your own front door. A pair of

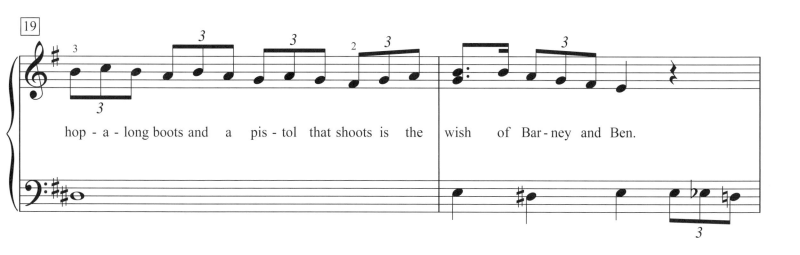

hop - a - long boots and a pis - tol that shoots is the wish of Bar - ney and Ben.

Dolls that will talk and will go for a walk is the hope of Jan - ice and Jen. And

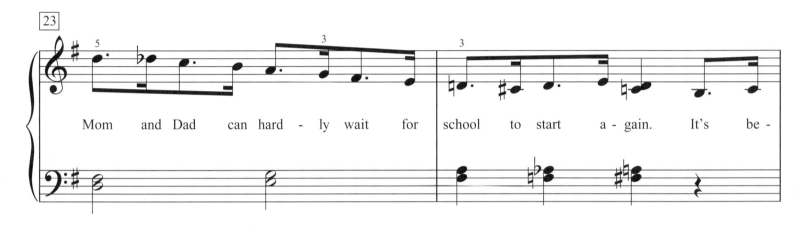

Mom and Dad can hard - ly wait for school to start a - gain. It's be -

gin - ning to look a lot like Christ - mas,

ev - 'ry - where you go. There's a tree in the Grand Ho - tel,

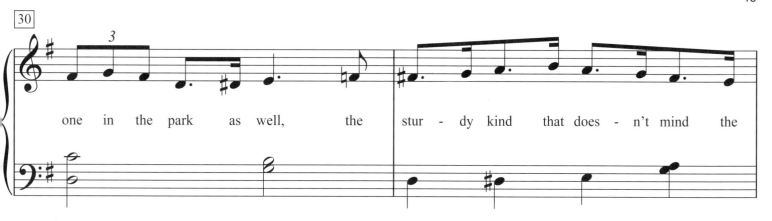

one in the park as well, the stur - dy kind that does - n't mind the

snow. It's be - gin-ning to look a lot like Christ - mas,

soon the bells will start. And the thing that will make them ring is the

car - ol that you sing right with - in your heart.

Let It Snow! Let It Snow! Let It Snow!

Words by SAMMY CAHN
Music by JULE STYNE

hate go-ing out in the storm; but if you'll real-ly hold me tight,

all the way home I'll be warm. The fire is slow-ly dy - ing, and my

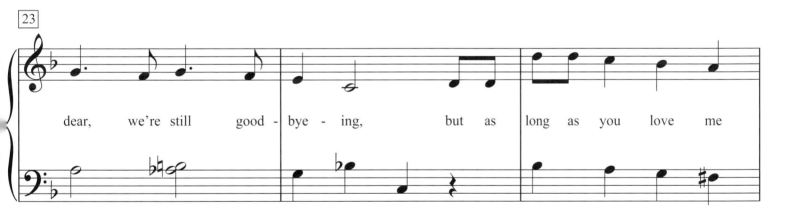

dear, we're still good - bye - ing, but as long as you love me

so, let it snow, let it snow, let it snow.

A Marshmallow World

Words by CARL SIGMAN
Music by PETER DE ROSE

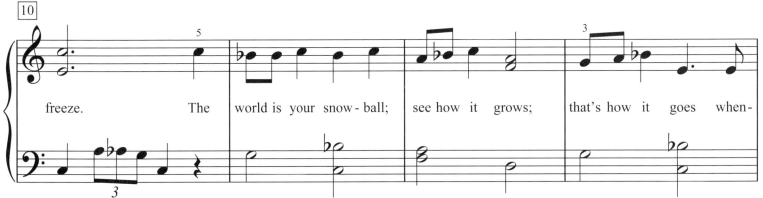

ev - er it snows. The world is your snow - ball; just for a song, get out and roll it a-

long. It's a yum, yum - my world made for sweet - hearts; ____ take a

walk with your fa - vor - ite girl. It's a sug - ar date; what if

spring is late? In win - ter, it's a marsh - mal - low world.

Mary, Did You Know?

Words and Music by MARK LOWRY
and BUDDY GREENE

by boy ___ has come to make ___ you new? This child ___
by boy ___ has walked where an - gels trod, and when you
by boy ___ was heav - en's per - fect Lamb, and the sleep -

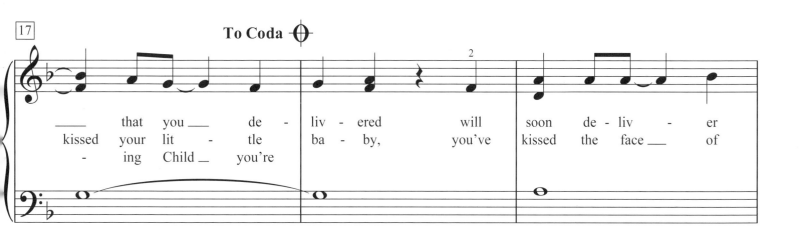

To Coda ⊕

___ that you ___ de - liv - ered will soon de - liv - er
kissed your lit - tle ba - by, you've kissed the face ___ of
- ing Child ___ you're

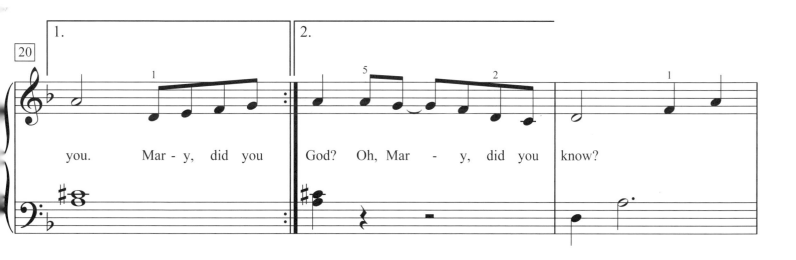

1.

2.

you. Mar - y, did you God? Oh, Mar - y, did you know?

The blind will see, ___ the

27

deaf will hear, __ the | dead will live __ a - | gain, the | lame will leap, __ the

31

D.S. al Coda

dumb will speak __ the | prais - es of __ the | Lamb. | Mar - y, did you

CODA

hold - ing is the | great | I | AM?

39

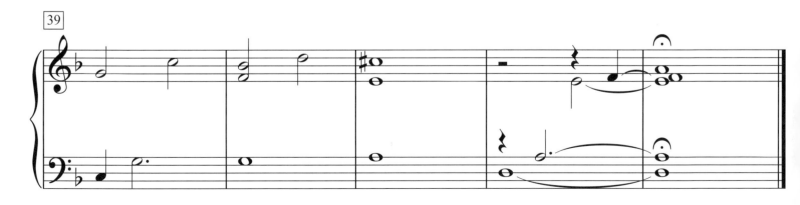

Rockin' Around the Christmas Tree

Music and Lyrics by
JOHNNY MARKS

Christ - mas tree, __ let the Christ - mas spir - it ring. __

Lat - er we'll have some pump - kin pie __ and we'll do some car - ol -

ing. You will get a sen - ti - men - tal feel - ing when you

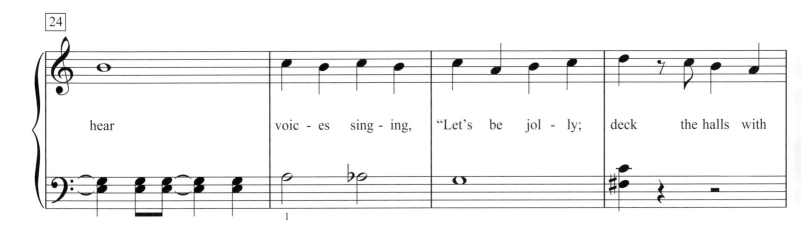

hear voic - es sing - ing, "Let's be jol - ly; deck the halls with

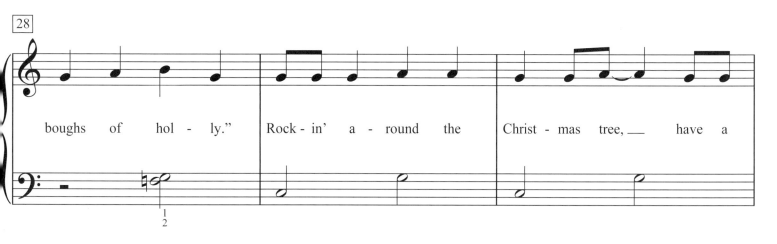

boughs of hol - ly." Rock - in' a - round the Christ - mas tree, ___ have a

hap - py hol - i - day. ___ Ev - 'ry - one danc - ing

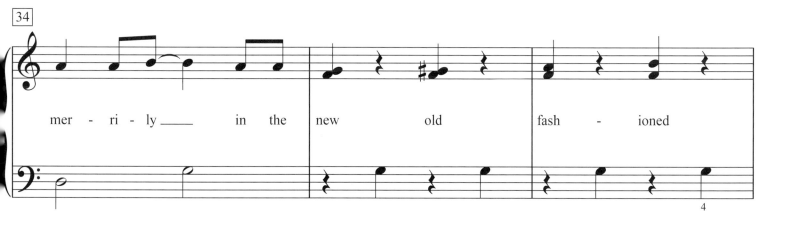

mer - ri - ly ___ in the new old fash - ioned

way.

The Most Wonderful Time of the Year

Words and Music by EDDIE POLA
and GEORGE WYLE

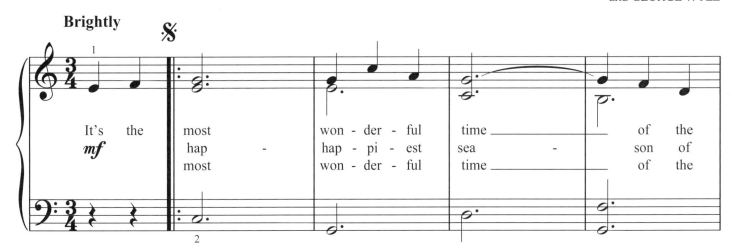

car - ol - ing out in the snow. _____ There'll be scar - y ghost

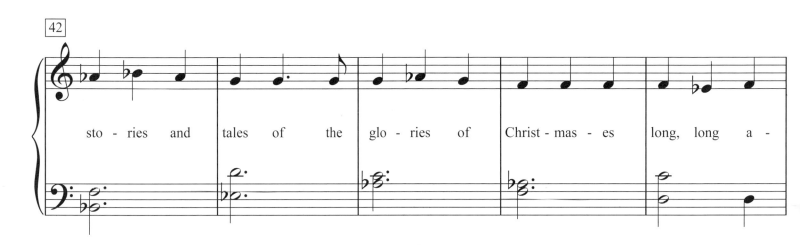

sto - ries and tales of the glo - ries of Christ - mas - es long, long a -

CODA

D.S. al Coda

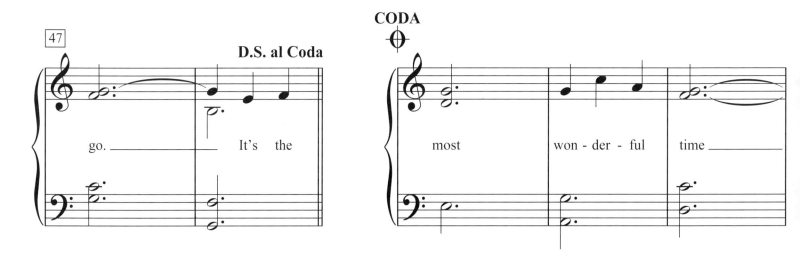

go. _____ It's the most won - der - ful time _____

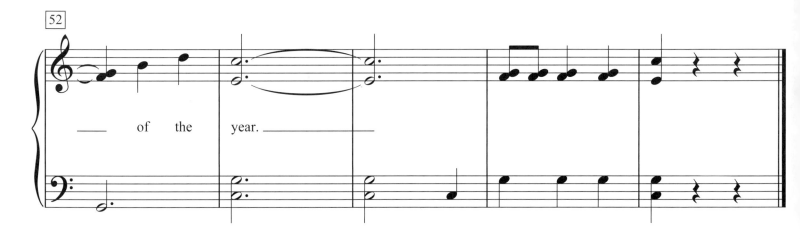

_____ of the year. _____

Santa Claus Is Comin' to Town

Words by HAVEN GILLESPIE
Music by J. FRED COOTS

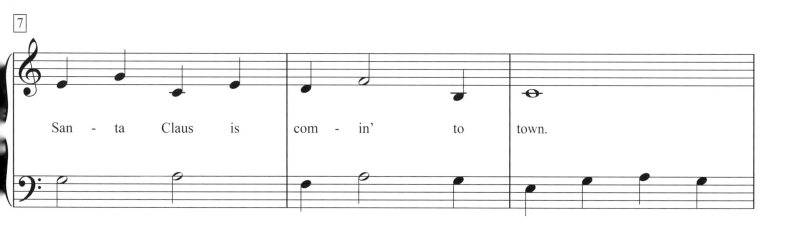

64

He's making a list and check-ing it twice,

gon-na find out who's naugh-ty and nice, San-ta Claus is

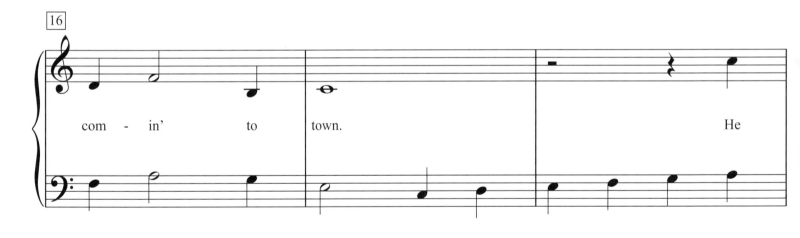

com - in' to town. He

sees you when you're sleep-in', he knows when you're a -

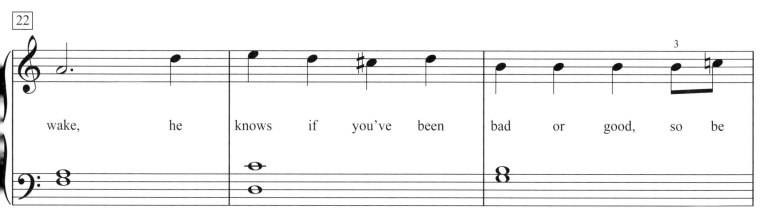

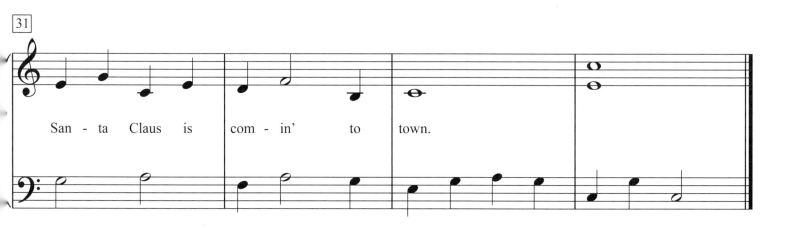

Rudolph the Red-Nosed Reindeer

Music and Lyrics by
JOHNNY MARKS

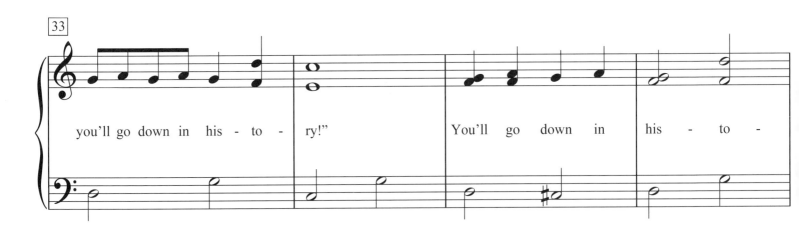

Silver Bells

from the Paramount Picture THE LEMON DROP KID

Words and Music by JAY LIVINGSTON
and RAY EVANS

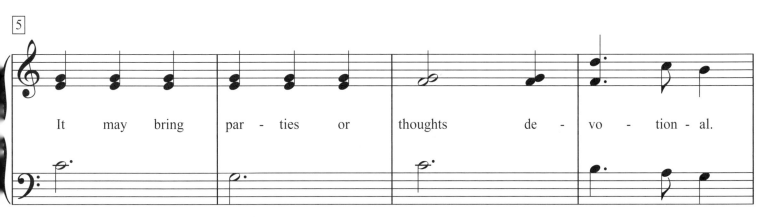

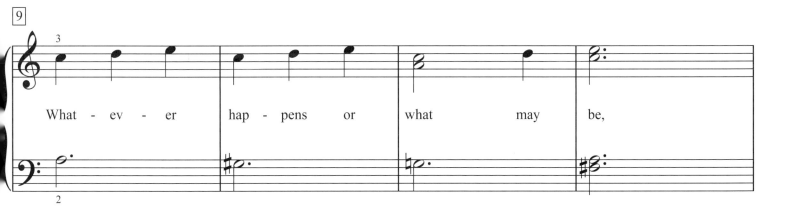

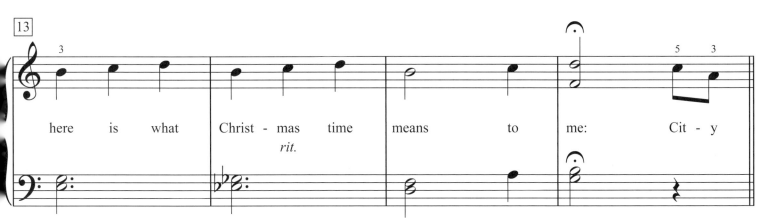

17 **Moderately**

side - walks, bus - y
street lights, e - ven

side - walks dressed in
stop - lights blink a

hol - i - day
bright red and

style. In the
green as the

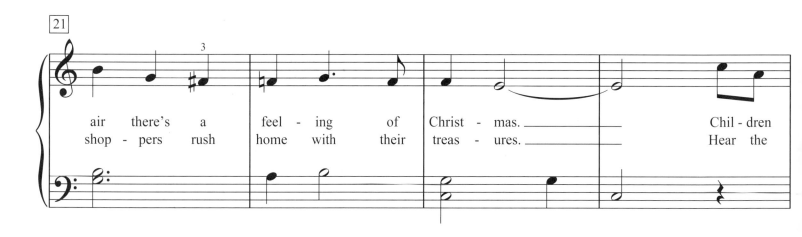

21

air there's a
shop - pers rush

feel - ing of
home with their

Christ - mas.
treas - ures.

Chil - dren
Hear the

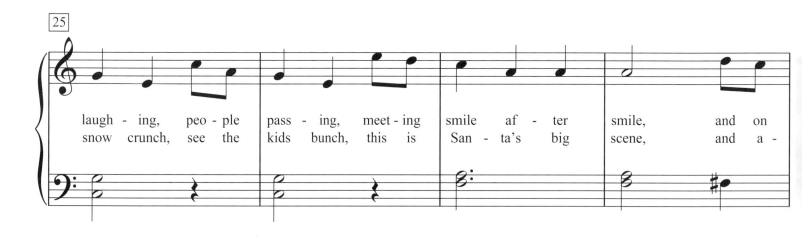

25

laugh - ing, peo - ple
snow crunch, see the

pass - ing, meet - ing
kids bunch, this is

smile af - ter
San - ta's big

smile, and on
scene, and a -

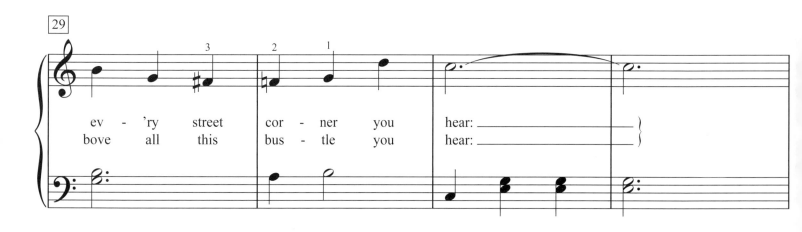

29

ev - 'ry street
bove all this

cor - ner you
bus - tle you

hear:
hear:

Sil - ver bells,   sil - ver bells,

it's Christ - mas   time   in the   cit - y. _____   Ring - a - ling,

hear them ring,   soon   it   will

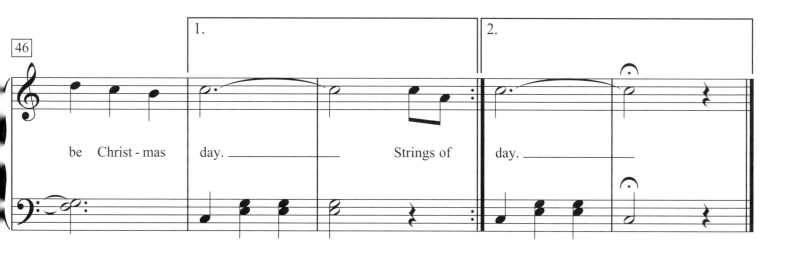

be Christ - mas   day. _____   Strings of   day. _____

Somewhere in My Memory

from the Twentieth Century Fox Motion Picture HOME ALONE

Words by LESLIE BRICUSSE
Music by JOHN WILLIAMS

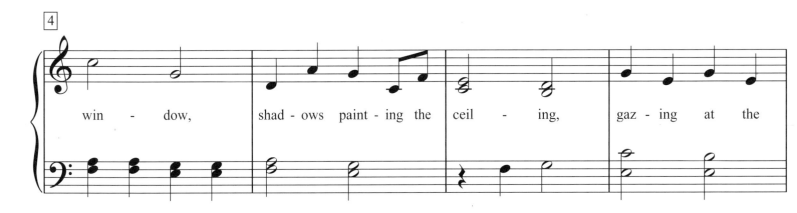

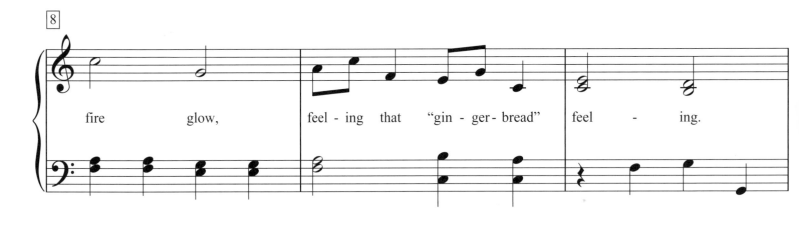

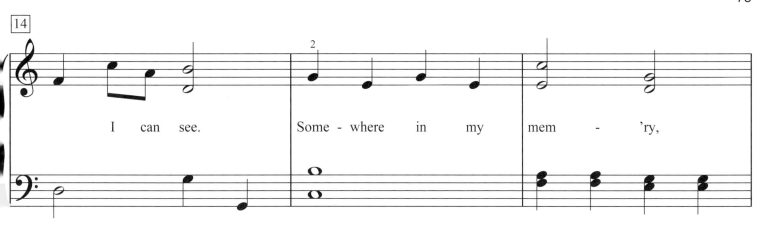

I can see. Some - where in my mem - 'ry,

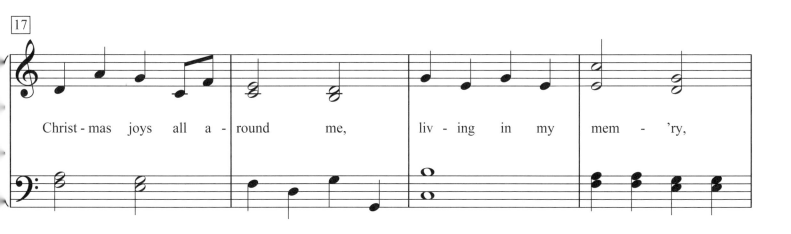

Christ - mas joys all a - round me, liv - ing in my mem - 'ry,

all of the mu - sic, all of the mag - ic, all of the fam - 'ly

home here with me.

Underneath the Tree

Words and Music by KELLY CLARKSON
and GREG KURSTIN

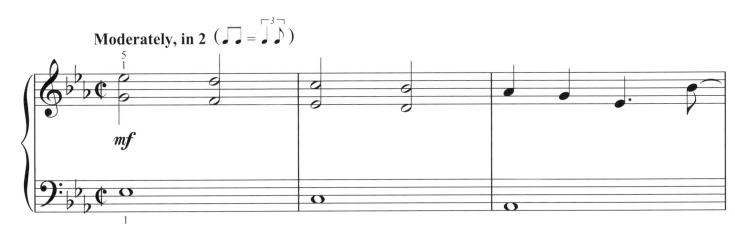

You're   here ___   where you should be. ___

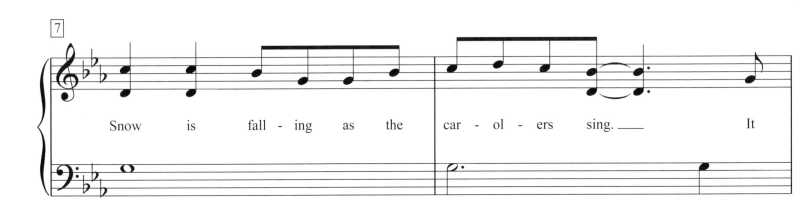

Snow   is   fall-ing   as   the   car-ol-ers   sing. ___   It

just was - n't the same ___ a - lone on Christ-mas Day. ___

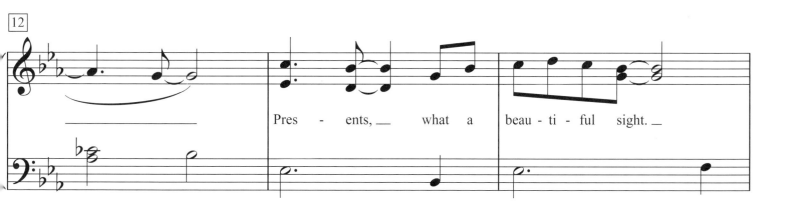

___ Pres - ents, ___ what a beau - ti - ful sight. ___

Don't mean a thing if you ain't hold - in' me tight. ___ You're all that I need ___

___ un - der - neath the tree ___ { to - night.
{ I've found ___

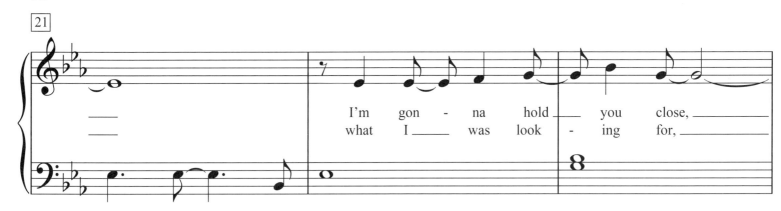

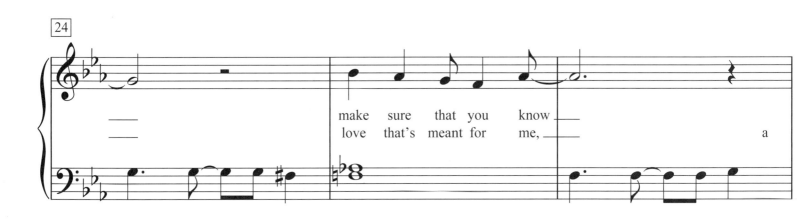

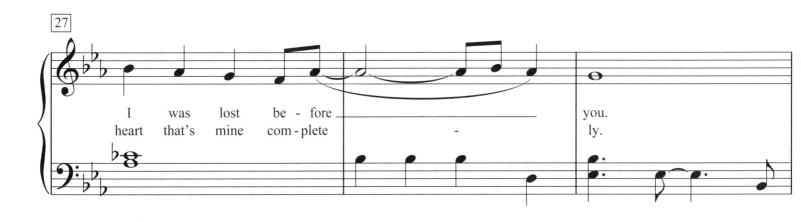

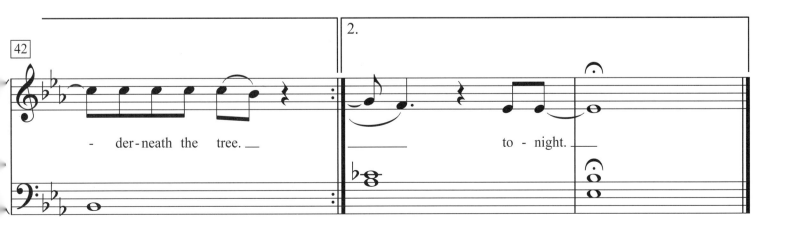

White Christmas

From the Motion Picture Irving Berlin's HOLIDAY INN

Words and Music by
IRVING BERLIN

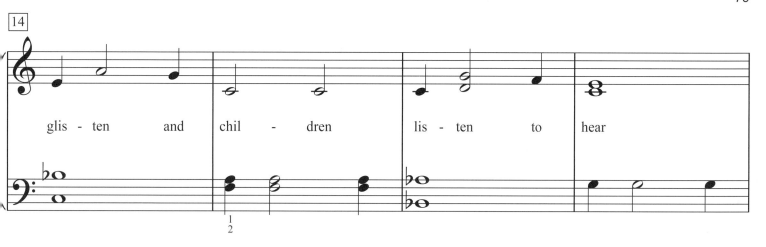

glis - ten and chil - dren lis - ten to hear

sleigh - bells in the snow.

I'm dream - ing of a white

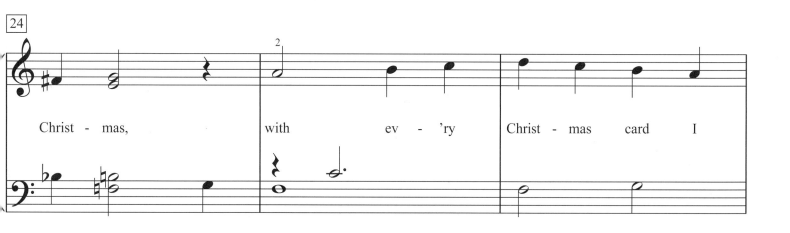

Christ - mas, with ev - 'ry Christ - mas card I

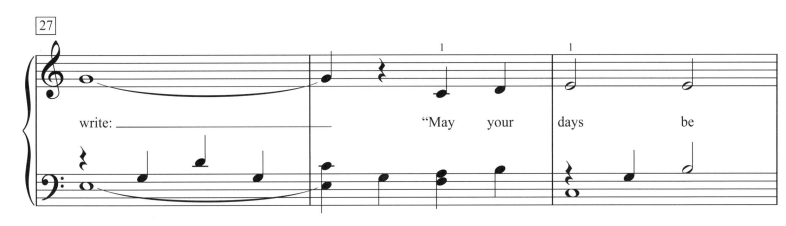

write: _____ "May your days be

mer - ry and bright _____ and may all your

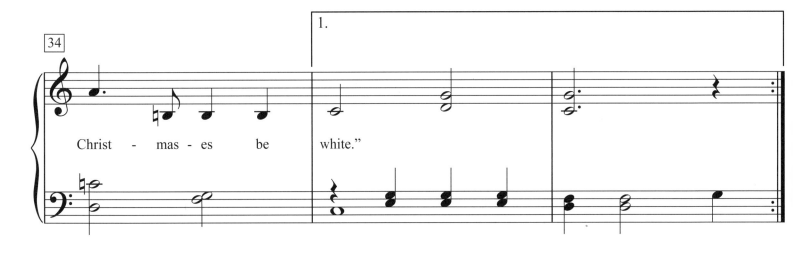

1.

Christ - mas - es be white."

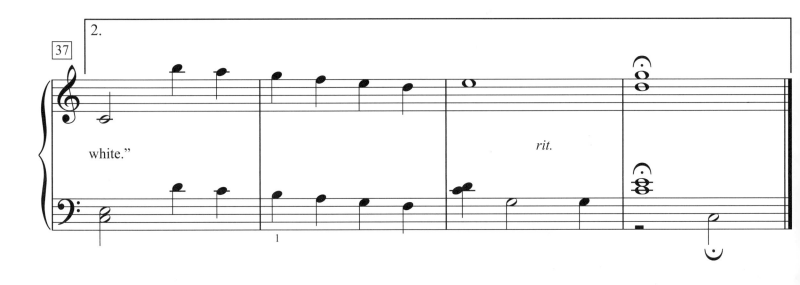

2.

white." *rit.*